Irwin Quagmire Wart
Travels to
PARIS, FRANCE

A kid's guide to the City of Lights

…by Irwin Quagmire Wart

I would like to express very special thanks to these people for helping to make this book possible:

The City of Paris, without her kindness and generosity of spirit, this book would have been impossible to write and photograph. I spent an incredible 10 days in this amazing city and it was love at first sight. This was my first trip abroad and I am so happy that not only was my book idea widely accepted, but that I survived the trip with both my legs still intact!

Pierre-Marie de Paris, for his excellent photography work as well as for his friendship, patience, and help as my tour guide and interpreter.

Greg Somerville for taking such good care of all the critters so that my favorite human (Elaine) and I could make this dream trip a reality.

Neva Lockett from Friends of the Buda (TX) Library for her help and words of encouragement.

My friends at the Tye Preston Library in Canyon Lake, TX for their help with my computer issues.

This book is dedicated to my human Auntie Kathy and Uncle Len for their unwavering support of my dream to became a writer and world traveler.
To all my family and friends in Land of Lily Pad. I hope this little book makes you proud.

My first frog was named "Rhumble." I received
him as a Christmas gift when I was very young. He inspired my
life-long love of frogs and, yes, even France. He made Irwin possible.

Elaine Rogers, Irwin's human (and secretary)

My Early Interest in Travel

I have always wanted to travel. Even as a young tadpole, I would venture far away from my school causing my teacher, Mr. McPhrogg, to worry about my safety. It wasn't that I was unhappy or didn't love my home and family, but I knew that that the Land of Lily Pad was just a small place and that the world was big and full of wonderful, exciting places. And I wanted to see them all. I read lots of books about far-away lands and spent too much time daydreaming that I was a famous explorer. My teacher would scold me and, for a while, I'd forget about traveling. But I had a dream; a dream that sooner or later, I knew I would have to follow.

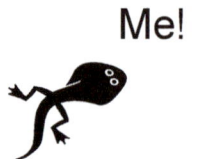

Me!

Chapter One – I Prepare For My Trip

When I got old enough, my teacher told me I would need a passport if I were going to travel to all those far-away places that I had dreamed about for so long. "A passport? What is that?", I asked Mr. McPhrogg. He explained to me that a passport was an official government document, issued by the country where you are a citizen. A passport allows you to travel to foreign countries and return again to your homeland.

I knew that before I could plan my first trip, I would need to apply for a passport. So I had a passport picture taken, filled out the application form and sent it, along with my birth certificate, to City of Swamp, the capital of Land of Lily Pad. A few weeks later, my very own passport arrived in the mail.

Once my passport arrived, I purchased an airline ticket to Paris, France and began planning my first trip! I was about to fulfill my dream. I was so excited, but I had things to do first before I could begin packing!

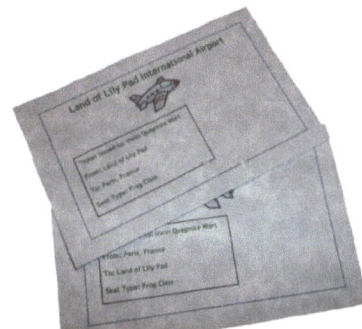

I went to the public library and, with the help of the librarian, I chose a few books about France, her people, and customs. The librarian suggested that I might want to use my home computer and do some additional research. I wanted to be well-prepared before I left on my amazing trip.

My researched showed that there weren't many travel books written for frogs, or children so I, Irwin Quagmire Wart, decided to write my own book while I was in Paris! That meant I needed to bring a note pad and, of course, my digital camera.

I learned many things that would be very helpful on my trip.

French, one of the romance languages, is the official language of the country. France is a very, very old country with a proud and rich history. The French flag is made of up three vertical bands of color; blue white, and red. The government of France is a Republic and is governed by a president, prime minister, national assembly, and senate. The motto of France is Liberty, Equality, Fraternity (brotherhood). This saying became popular during the French revolution of 1789 but was not recognized at the official motto until the end of the 19th century.

The flag of France

France is the largest country in the European Union. (Shown in blue on the map below.) Many of the countries in the European Union, including France, use a currency (money) called the Euro. Paris is the capital of France. It is also the largest city in that country. Paris is located on the banks of the River Seine in the northern part of France and is the most visited city in the whole world! Paris is often called The City of Lights. Paris is home to many famous monuments, museums, cathedrals, and gardens. And I wanted to see them all!

EU money or "Euros". The symbol for euros is a C with two lines through it

The countries in blue make up the European Union, or EU, as it's commonly called.

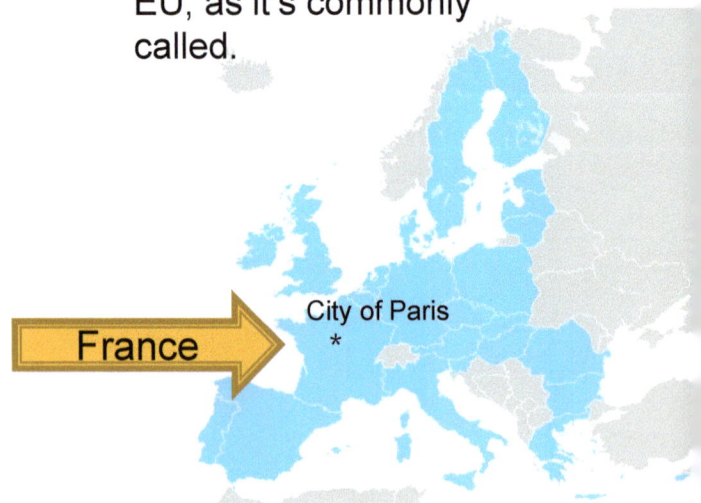

France

City of Paris
*

Now that my research was finished and I was all packed, the day finally arrived for me to begin my trip. I wanted to see everything and was anxious to begin my Paris adventure! I double-checked that I had everything, including my passport, ticket, and my camera. I couldn't believe that I, Irwin Quagmire Wart, was finally ready to take my first trip. So, with my passport in my flipper, I said goodbye to all my friends, kissed my parents farewell, then set off for the Land of Lilly Pad International Airport. I was on my way at last!

Irwin Learns French

hi/bye – salut   (sa-loo)

goodbye – au revoir (ohr-vwahr)

See you later – à bientôt   (ah bee-an-toe)

please – s'il vous plait   (see voo play)

thank you – merci   (mehr-see)

yes – oui   (wee)

no – non (noh)

Irwin Learns French

one – un   (ahn)

two – deux   (duh)

three – trois   (trwah)

four – quatre   (kahtr)

five – cinq (sank)

six – six (sees)

seven – sept (seht)

eight – huit   (weet)

nine – neuf   (nuhf)

ten – dix   (dees)

Chapter Two – I Arrive in Paris

It was a long flight. Once I arrived in Paris and got settled in at my hotel, I set off to see the sites. I found that there were several ways to see Paris: By tourist boat,

by double-decker site seeing bus,

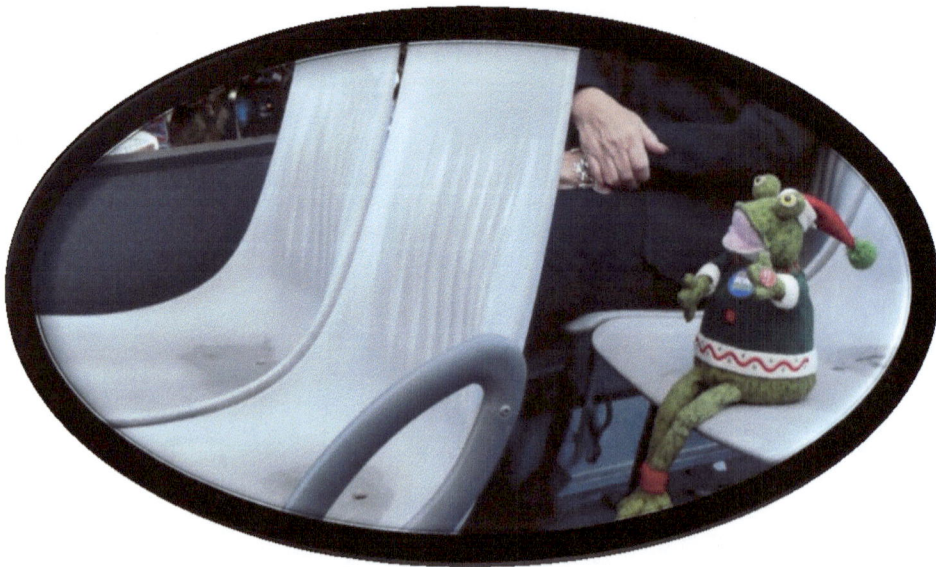

and by hopping, I mean foot. I decided that I liked hopping the best. There's always lots to see, no matter where you stop to rest. The River Seine runs through the center of the city, creating the Right Bank and Left Bank of Paris. The left bank is the south side of the river and right bank in the north side of the river. Here, I am resting on the Left Bank.

Beautiful and colorful carousels for children, and frogs, of all ages to enjoy can be found all over Paris.

I'm having so much fun!

Can you think of another name for a carousel?
(See page 80 for the answer)

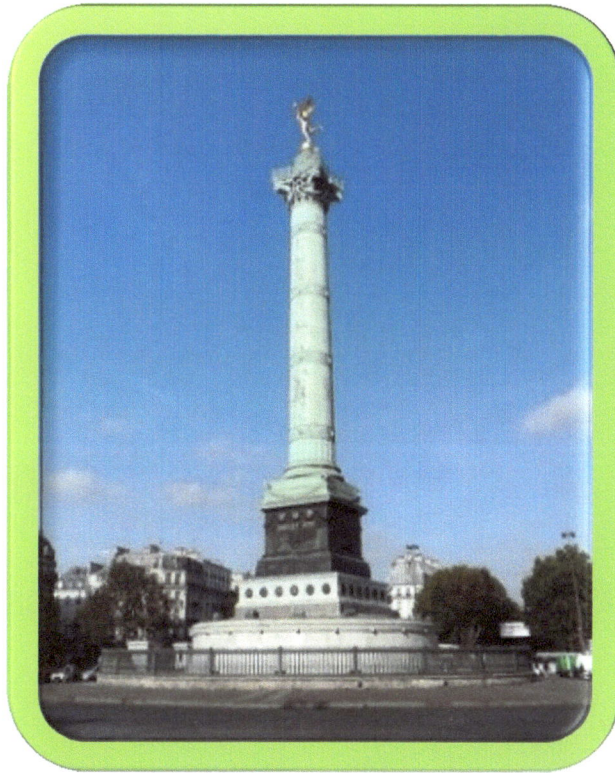

This is Bastille Square in Paris, and it commemorates the place where the famous French Revolution started on July 14, 1789. The monument is called the July Column or colonne de juillet in French.

It's been a very busy day so I think I'll head back to my hotel for a dinner of French flies (mouches français in French) and a big glass of swamp water. YUM!

Irwin Learns French

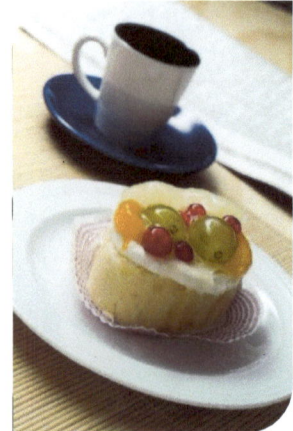

breakfast – le petit déjeuner   (luh puh-tee day-zhun-nay)

lunch – le déjeuner   (luh day-zhun-nay)

dinner – le diner   (luh deenay)

milk – lait   (lay)

coffee – café (kah-fay)

tea – thé   (tay)

pastry – patisserie   (pah-tees-ree)

bread – pain   (pahn)

Chapter 3 – Day 2 in Paris

Another beautiful day in this amazing city. I have so much more to see.

I learned that the original city of Paris was built on an island in the middle of the River Seine. Behind me you can see one of the two islands, named Île Saint Louis Cité (island of City of Saint Louis), and the bridge that connects it to the mainland.

Everywhere I went, there were wonderful things to see. I spotted these two cats on a roof in the Saint-Jacques Tower Garden, one of the oldest and most famous gardens in Paris.

There are many large and beautiful statues in Paris. I decided to rest at this one located near the entrance to the Orsay Museum. This museum is home to many works of art from the Impressionist period (1867 to 1886) and includes works from Monet, Renoir, and Degas...to name a few.

This is a very large elephant, and I'm only a very small frog!

Irwin Learns French

January – janvier (zhan-vee-ay)
February – février (fay-vree-ay)
March – mars   (mahrs)
April – avril (ah-vreel)
May – mai   (meh)
June – juin (zhwahn)
July – juliet   (zhwee-yeh)
 August – août   (oot)
September – septembre   (sehp-tahm-bre)
October – octobre   (ok-tohbre)
November – novembre   (noh-vahmbre)
December – décembre   (day-sahmbre)

Generally, in French, the names of months are not
capitalized, unless they are the first word in a sentence.

Chapter Four – Day 3 in Paris

Today I am only going to visit one museum. It is very large and will take me most of the day to see all that I want to see. The Musée (mew-zay) de Louvre (loov) , as it is called in French, is one of the largest and most visited museums in the entire world. It is home to many famous works of art. Originally the Louvre was a palace, but it became a public museum at the end of the 1700's.

Located in the Louvre courtyard, this new museum entrance was constructed in 1989 by architect I.M. Pei (Pay). It is often referred to as the Pei Pyramid. Made out of glass and steel, the structure allows sunlight to come in to the underground floor.

I am very excited to see everything that's inside!

This 1930's American Buick automobile, that has been converted into a modern-day low-rider, is in the lobby of the Louvre Museum.

I wish I was tall enough to drive!

Lucky me! Here I'm standing in front of the "Mona Lisa" painting at The Louvre Museum. This is the most famous painting in the world . Mona Lisa was painted by an Italian artist named Leonardo Da Vinci. It took him from 1503 to 1519 to complete this work of art. Great works of art are often called "masterpieces".

My first "selfie"

Why do you think the Mona Lisa is smiling?

Here, I take a few minutes to enjoy some of the amazing works of art that are on display here at the Musée de Louvre (and to rest my little froggy legs). I can't believe how many paintings there are to see!

Venus de Milo

Winged Victory

I can't decide which statue I like the best

This extraordinary statue was discovered in Greece in 1820. It is believed to have been carved between 130 and 100 BC. The statue depicts Aphrodite, or Venus, the goddess of love.

"Winged Victory" as this statue is named, is one of the most celebrated sculptures in the Louvre. It depicts the Greek goddess Nike, which means victory.
The statue was discovered in April of 1863. It is believed to have been carved in the second century BC.

Egyptian Antiquities at the Louvre

Me and the sphinx

The Egyptian Collection at the Louvre was begun by Emperor Napoleon 1. It covers the civilization found in the Nile River Valley from 5000 BC to 400 AD.

An Egyptian Sarcophagus, which is similar to a coffin, is usually carved out of stone.

After spending many hours here at the Louvre, I have only scratched the surface of all there is to see. The rest of its treasures will have to wait for another trip to Paris.

The sun is shining and it's a beautiful day. Just outside of the Louvre, is one of the prettiest gardens in all of Paris. That will be the perfect place to relax and catch a few bugs for my lunch.

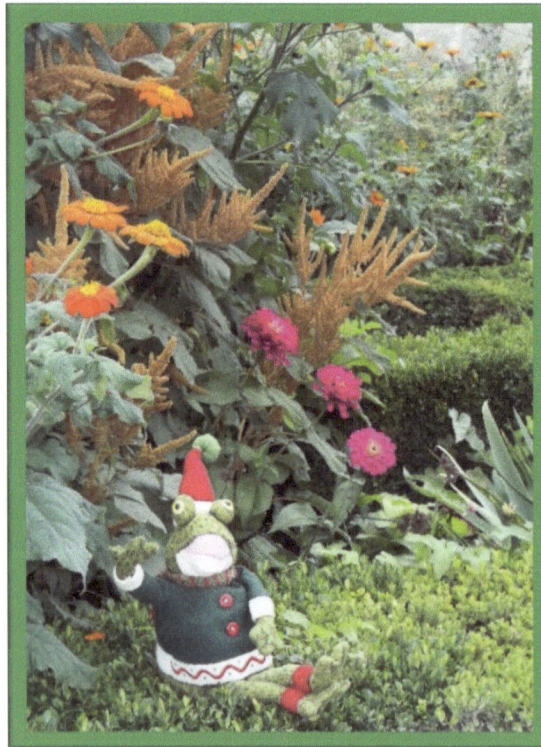

Did you know that the City of Paris has over 400 public gardens? With so many gardens and parks, Paris is the most wooded and green capital city in all of Europe!

Tuileries (Twill-er-ee) gardens are located very near the Louvre Museum. Originally, it was the private garden for the Tuileries Palace in 1564. In 1667, the gardens were opened to the public and, after the French Revolution of 1789, the gardens became a public park. This amazing (and HUGE) garden is also home to the Musée de l'Orangerie (mew-zay de l'or-ahn-ger-ee). This museum is a showcase for many of the paintings by the famous French artist Claude Monet (Mo-nay).

After a very busy day, I decide to head back to my hotel. Once there, I take time to learn a little more French. After dinner I relax, then fall into a deep sleep. I am very tired, but excited about seeing more of Paris. Each day seems to be better than the last. What an amazing time I'm having. I'm one lucky little frog!

Irwin Learns French

my father – mon père
(mow pehr)

grandmother – grand-mere (grahn-mehr)

grandfather – grand-père (grahn-pehr)

cousins – cousins (koo-zen)

aunt – tante   (tahnt)

uncle – oncle   (ohncle)

my mother – ma
mere (mah-mehr)

me – moi
(mwa)

My friends – mes amis
(mays ah-mee)

Irwin Learns French

red – rouge   (roozh)

green – vert (vehr)

blue – bleu   (bluh)

yellow – jaune   (zhon)

orange – orange   (Oh-ranzh

black – noir   (nwahr)

white – blanc   (blahn)

brown – marron   (mah-rohn)

Chapter 5 – Day 4 in Paris

The Notre Dame de Paris (no-tre Dahm de Paree) Cathedral was begun in 1163 and continued, on and off, until it's completion in 1345. The name, in French, means Our Lady of Paris .

It is the most visited site in Paris. To get to the top of the tower, where the great bell is located, I had to hop up nearly 400 stairs!

Once at the top, I could see the whole city and the River Seine far below me.

Here I am sitting atop one of the towers at Notre Dame.

The great bell, in the south bell tower, is named Emmanuelle. It is only rung on special occasions. It was cast (made) over 300 years ago.

Here I am among the chimeras on top of Notre Dame Cathedral. A chimera is a carved stone figure, grotesque or mythical, usually made of granite and used for decorative purposes.

I can see many of the places I've already visited from way up here!

The North Rose Window at Notre Dame was constructed in 1250 and still contains most of the original glass. Isn't it beautiful? And it's so BIG!

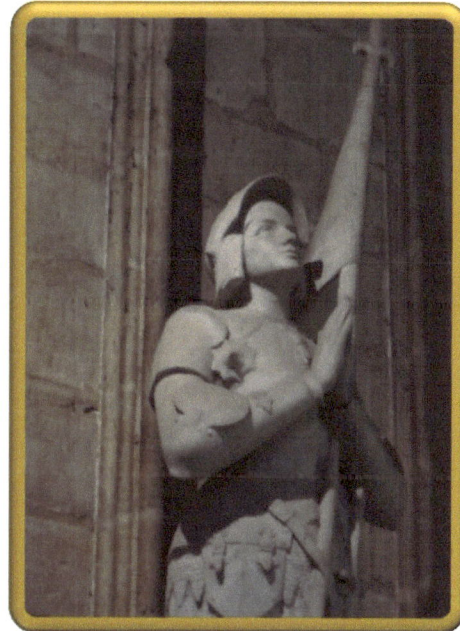

Inside Notre Dame Cathedral are many statues, like this one of Joan of Arc.

Point Zero, located in the Notre Dame courtyard, is the exact center of Paris. It is the official point from where all distances in France are measured from.

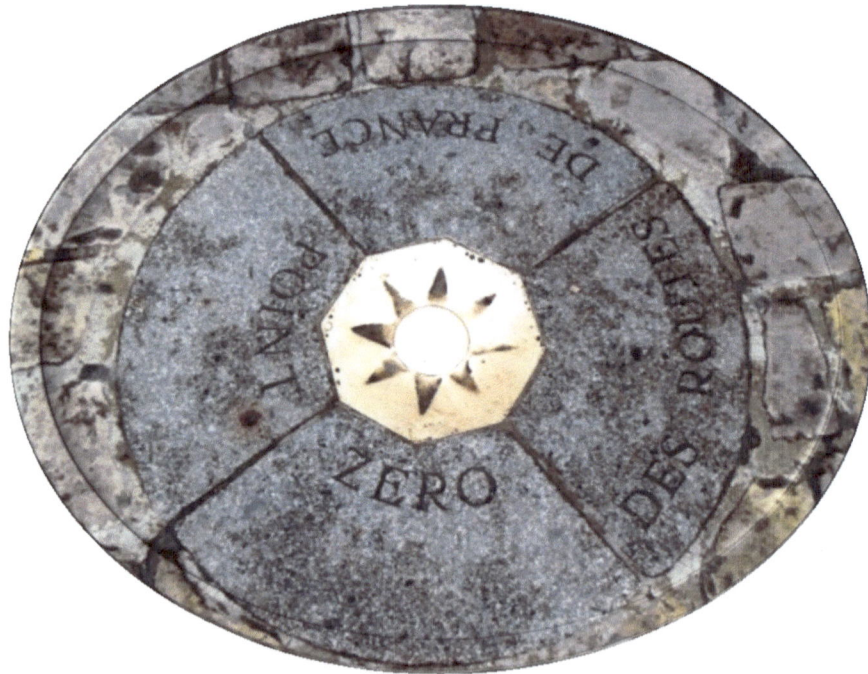

Once I had finished visiting Notre Dame, I hopped over to see the most famous bookstore in all of Paris.

Shakespeare and Company was the first English-language bookstore to open in Paris. The first location opened its doors in 1919 and moved to this larger shop in 1922, where it's visited by thousands of book lovers, like me, every year.

During the 1920's the bookstore became a gathering place for many famous authors of the day; Ezra Pound, James Joyce, and Ernest Hemingway, to name just a few.

Since I love to read, I hopped up the tiny, narrow staircase and found this cozy chair to sit in while I leafed through many of the old and rare books that are for sale here. Maybe one day, my books will be sold here!

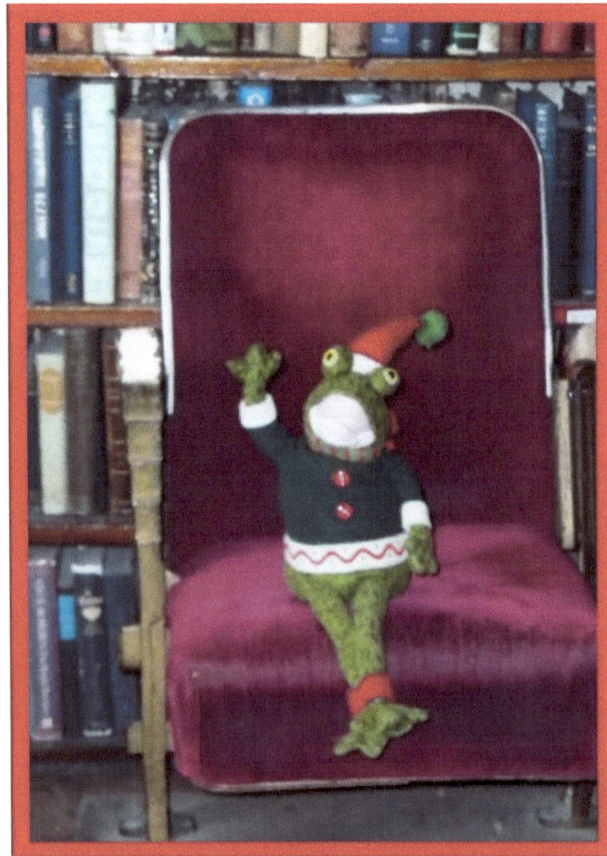

Irwin Learns to Speak French

Monday – lundi (lun-dee)

Tuesday – mardi (mahr-dee)

Wednesday – mercredi (mehr-cre-dee)

Thursday – jeudi (juh-dee)

Friday – vendredi (vahn-druh-dee)

Saturday- samedi (sahm-dee)

Sunday – dimadche (dee-mahnsh)

As in the months of the year, the days of the week are generally not capitalized in French, unless they are the first word in a sentence.

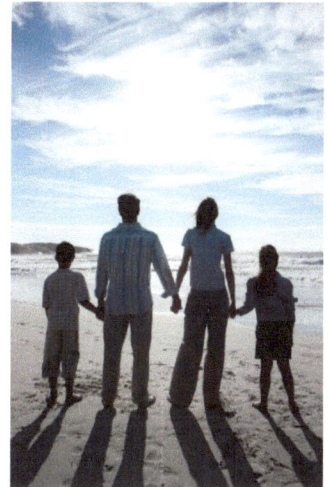

Chapter 6 – Day 5 in Paris

In Paris, art is everywhere and I saw many wonderful examples just by hopping along the quaint streets and boulevards.

Here I look like part of the artwork!

This is one of the coolest things I saw on my trip. Marcel Aymé (Amee), a famous French novelist and children's author (1902-1967) wrote a short story entitled *Le Passe-Muraille* (le pas-se meur-eye) or *The Walker-Through-Walls*. This is a statue of that story's main character. Maybe one day, if I become a famous author too, there will be a statue of me in Paris!

Me

There are amazing fountains of every kind.

There are so many fun things to see, just by hopping around this city. It's been a full day of sightseeing and I decide it's time to go back to my hotel. I can't wait until tomorrow….

Chapter 7 – Day 6 in Paris

Today I am going to the Eiffel Tower or Tour Eiffel as it's called in French. Originally built in 1889 for the World Exposition, the Eiffel Tower is the most famous landmark in the world! It can be seen from many places in Paris. The Eiffel Tower is located on the Champs de Mars (sha de mars). It was designed and built by Gustave Eiffel. It stands 1,063' tall, that's 324 meters in metric. There are over 700 stairs up to the top.

My little froggy legs were very tired when I got to the top, but the view was well worth the effort.

All of Paris lay before me!

At night, it lights up the evening sky!

I am at the very tippy top of this famous monument.

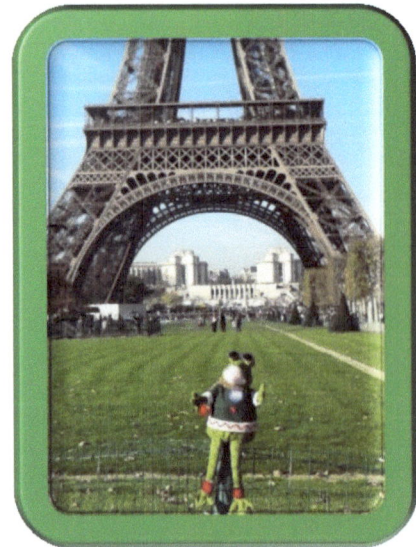

I'm sitting right in front of the Eiffel Tower!

Can You Draw the Eiffel Tower?

Ask for a sheet of paper and a pencil, pen, or crayon and see if you can draw it better than me. I bet you can! Do you think my drawing will be exhibited in the Louvre Museum one day? Maybe yours will!

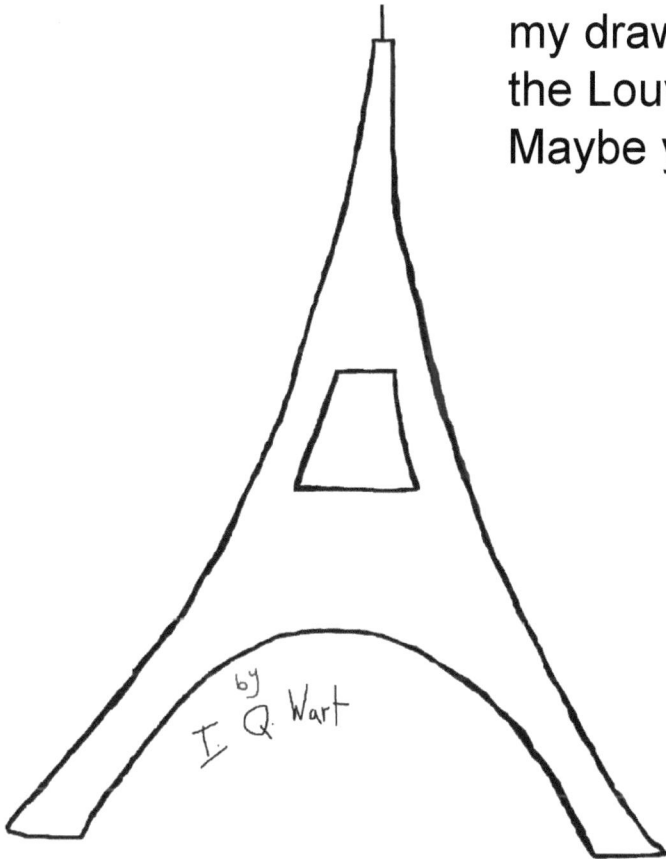

by
I. Q. Wart

What would a trip to Paris be without a stop at a sidewalk café? So, before heading back to my hotel, I decided to stop and enjoy a cup of hot chocolate. It was the perfect way to end a perfect day in Paris!

Irwin Learns French

dog - chien (male) she-ah or
chienne (female) she-ahn)

cat - chat (male) shah or
chatte -female (shaht)

bird – oiseau   (wa-zo)

rabbit – lapin   (la-pah)

frog – grenouille   (greh-nwee-yuh)

duck – canard   (kah-nar)

cow – vache   (vash)

pig – cochon   (ko-shah)

teacher - professeur
male (le pro-feh-suhr)
female (lah pro-feh-suhr)

HELP DESK

librarian – bibliothécaire
(bib-lee-o-tay-care)

Irwin Leans French

school – école (ay-kole)

library – bibliothèque
(bib-lee-o-tehk)

pen – le stylo (le stee-lo)

pencil – crayon (kray-yoh)

paper – papier (pahp-yay)

books – livres (leev-rah)

computer – ordinateur
(ohr-din-a-tewr)

students – étudians
(ay-to0-dee-ahn)

school bus – autobus scolaire
(auto-bous skoh-lare)

Chapter 8 – Day 7 in Paris

me

This is a replica of the Statue of Liberty found on Liberty Island in New York City. The original statue was a gift of friendship, given to the people of the United States of America from the people of France.

Below is a replica of Liberty's flame. It was given to the City of Paris by the International Herald Tribune newspaper in 1989. It stands 11 feet tall, that's 3.5 meters.

me

The City of Paris has 37 bridges that cross the River Seine. Four of them are used by people only. The oldest bridge is Pont Neuf, which means new bridge. It was originally built in 1607.

The bridge Pont des Arts (bridge of the arts) became a living memorial to the true love of the many couples who visited this romantic city. After the "lovelock" was placed on the bridge, the couple then threw the keys into the River Seine below, thus locking their love for each other, and Paris, to the bridge forever. Over time, so many locks were placed on the bridge that the extra weight made the bridge unsafe and the City of Paris had to remove them!

Street entertainers are common all over Paris. Whether it's musicians, artists, jugglers, or puppeteers, like this young lady, there are always free shows to watch.

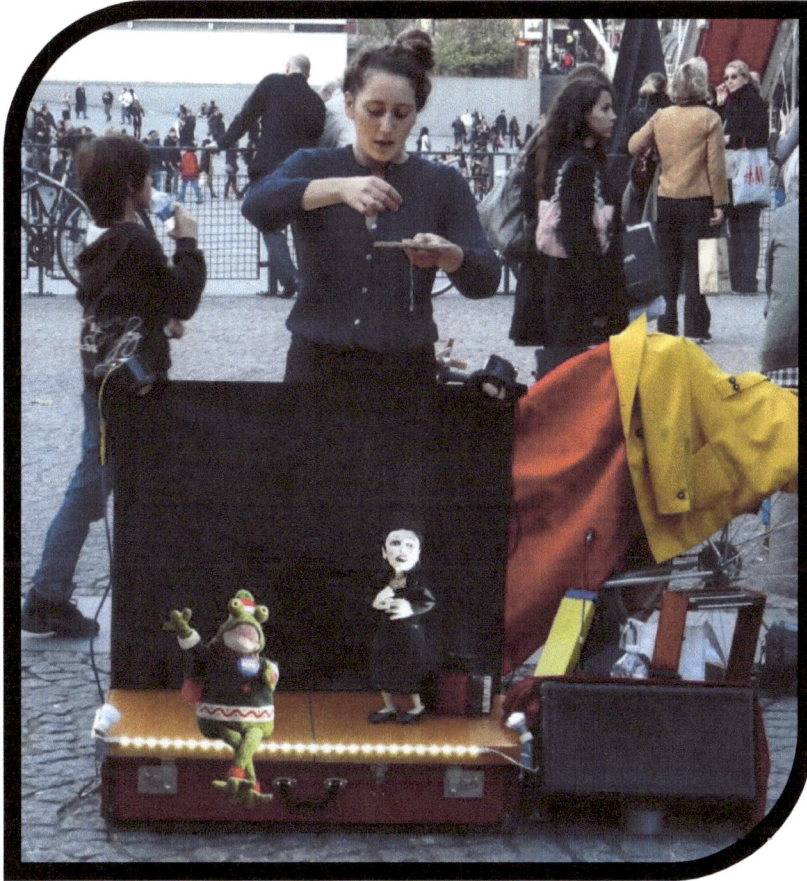

What is another name for a puppet with strings?
(See page 80 for the answer)

Other street entertainers include musicians, like this harpist and the "statue man" outside of the Basilique Sacré – Cœur (ba-sil-eek sa-cray- coor), which means Sacred Heart Basilica.

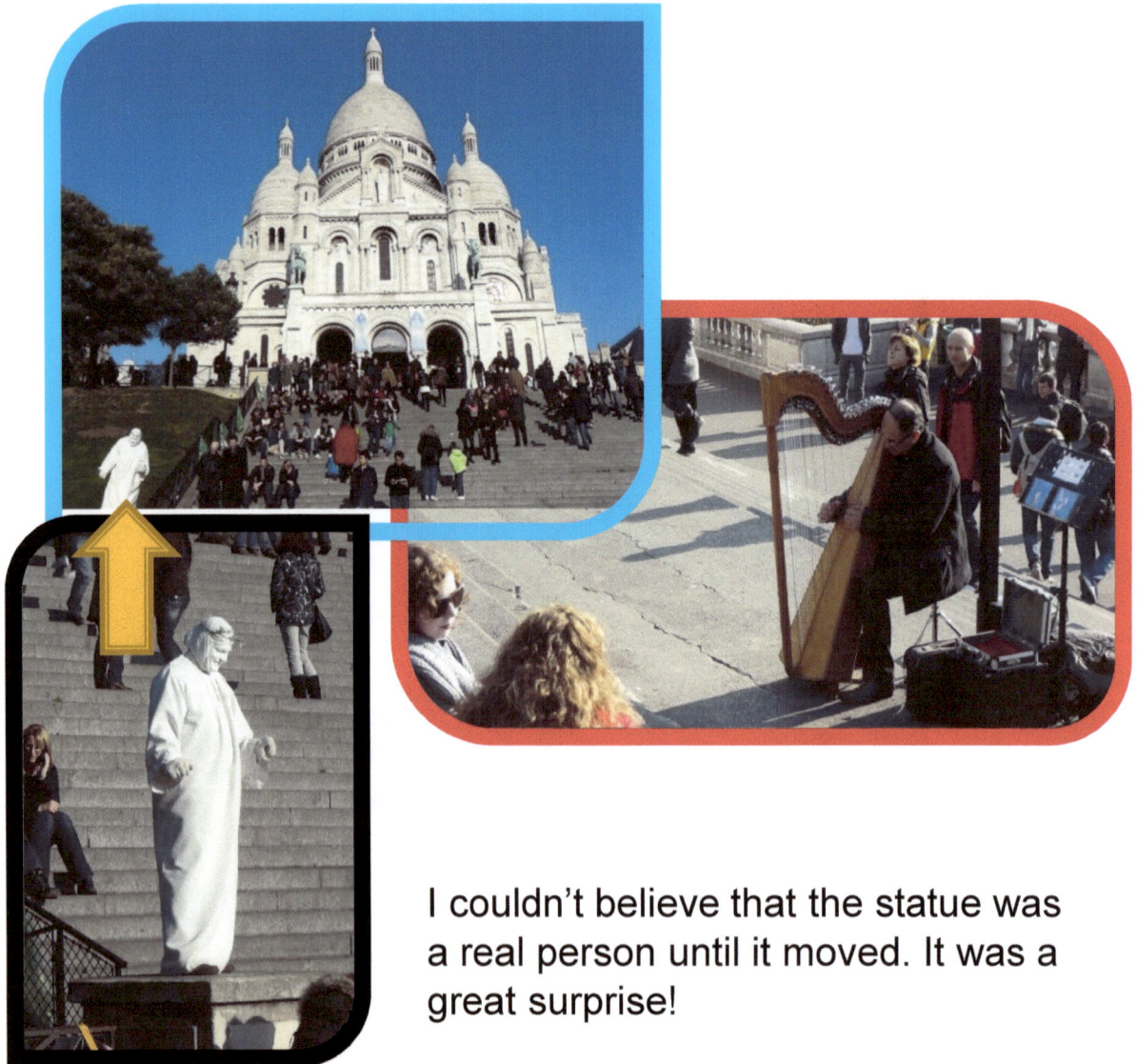

I couldn't believe that the statue was a real person until it moved. It was a great surprise!

Many old buildings, like Basilique Sacré-Cœur, (ba-zee-leek sah-kray-kohr) have gargoyles on top.

A gargoyle is very much like the chimeras I saw atop Notre Dame. It is usually made of granite and depicts an animal or other figure. Unlike the chimera, which is for decoration only, a gargoyle is used to drain water off the roofs of building. Notice the water trough in the goat's back. The open mouth is where the rain drains out onto the street below.

Irwin Learns French

north – nord   (nohr)

south – sud   (sood)

east – est (just it sounds)

west – ouest   (oo-est)

 Train ticket – billet de train
(bee-yeh de trah)

train station – gare (gahr)

car – voiture
(vwah-chewr)

Irwin Learns French

My name is - Je m'appellee
(zhuh ma-pehl)

How are you? - Comment vas-tu?
(kohmah vah-tew)

I'm OK. - Ca va.   (sah-vah)

I'm fine, thank you. - Ca va bien, merci.
(sah-vah be-an mehr-see)

And you? - Et Toi?
(ay twah)

Chapter 9 – Day 8 in Paris

This is the famed Champs- Élysées (shah zay-lee-zay). Behind me is the Arc de Triomphe or Arch of Triumph (ark duh tree-awmf).

In French, it's called Arc de Triomphe. It was commissioned by the emperor Napoleon I in 1806 to commemorate his victories. Since there isn't an elevator, or lift as it's called in Europe, I had to hop up 234 stairs to the observation deck at the top. Whew!

I actually got to meet a published author while I was in Paris. Olivier Magny (O-liv-ee-ay Mahn-yay), my new friend, autographed a copy of his book for me and posed for this cute picture!

The Paris Opera House, also called the Palais Garnier, (pa-lay ga-neyay was opened to the public in 1875.

Isn't this building beautiful? It is decorated with galleries, statues, and columns.

I'm sitting here in front of the Opera House and watching the Parisians stroll by. Parisian is the name for a person who lives in Paris.

Since I am visiting Paris in November, I decided to spend part of my last day in this enchanting city, seeing the beautiful Christmas decorations in the Galeries Lafayette. The Layfette Galleries is a large French department store that covers 10 floors! The store window displays, during the Christmas season, are a wonderland for children, and frogs, of all ages!

Each window's display was better than the one before. They were so amazing!

After I saw the spectacular Christmas Tree in the foyer of this huge shopping center on Boulevard Haussmann, it was time for me to head back to my hotel and prepare for the trip back home, to the Land of Lily Pad. Joyeux Noel (zwhy-you noh-well), in French, means Happy Christmas!

Irwin Learns French

hello/good day/good morning – bonjour
(bohn-zhoor)

good evening – bonsoir
(bohn-swahr)

good afternoon – bon apres midi
(bohn- ahpray- meedee)

good night – bonne nuit
(bohn-ne-wee)

Chapter 10 – I leave for home

As I flew home, I reflected back on my first trip. There were so many wonderful things to see and do, I couldn't decide which was the best. This trip was a dream come true and I hoped that I'd be able to visit many other exciting countries. "But", I thought to myself, "It will be good to get home to my parents and my friends." I had really missed them!

When I got home, I was very tired from the long trip. Happy to be back in my own little bed, I fell off to sleep and dreamed about my next big adventure….

Here's a fun little quiz that you can take to see how much you remember about my trip.
(I bet you can remember lots!)

Quiz Questions

1. France is the largest country in the _____ _____.
2. What is the capital of France?
3. What is a passport?
4. What are Euros?
5. What are the French words for hello and thank you?
6. What is the French word for lunch?
7. How do you say April in French?
8. The River _____runs through the center of Paris.
9. The French Revolution of 1789 took place in _____ Square.
10. What is the name of the largest museum in the world?
11. What famous painting of a smiling lady did I see?
12. I saw two famous Greek statues at the Louvre. They are the _____ de _____ and _____ _____
13. What is a chimera? Where did I pose with one?
14. What is the French phrase for "my mother"?

Quiz Questions

15. What is the most visited site in Paris?
16. What is "Point Zero"?
17. What is the French word for west?
18. What is the most famous landmark in the world and when was it built?
19. What is the French word for frog?
20. Can you count from 1 – 10 in French?
21. Who built the Arc de Triomphe?
22. What is the French word for teacher?
23. Mes amis means what in French?
24. Where is my home?

Answers to Quiz Questions

Page 16 – A carousel is also called a merry-go-round
Page 61 - A puppet with strings is called a marionette.

1. European Union
2. France
3. An official document that allows you to travel to another country and return home again.
4. Euros are the currency used in many of the countries in the European Union
5. Hello is bonjour. Thank you is merci
6. Lunch in French is dejeauner
7. April is Avril in French.
8. River Seine
9. Bastille Square
10. Musee de Louvre or The Louvre Museum.
11. Mona Lisa
12. The Venus de Milo and Winged Victory
13. A chimera is a grotesque or mythical carved, stone figure. I posed with one atop the Notre Dame Cathedral.
14. My mother, in French, is ma mere.

Answers to Quiz Questions

15. The most visited site is Notre Dame Cathedral.
16. Point Zero is the exact center of Paris. It is the point from which all official distance is measured.
17. The French word for west is ouest.
18. The most famous landmark in the world is the Tour Eiffel. It was built in 1889.
18. The French word for frog is grenouille.
20. Un, deux, trois, quatre, cinq, sis, sept, huit, neuf, dix.
21. Napoleon I built the Arc de Triomphe.
22. Teacher in French, is professeur.
23. Mes amis means my friends.
24. I live in the Land of Lily Pad.

Good Job. Well done!

About Irwin

Irwin currently lives near Austin, Texas with his personal assistant. Irwin's favorite color is green. His favorite foods are flies and mosquitoes. In his spare time, Irwin enjoys swimming, traveling, reading, writing, and spending time in the Land of Lily Pad with his family and friends. You can write to Irwin at Irwin@irwinquagmirewart.com. Be sure to visit his website at www.irwinquagmirewart.com! Follow Irwin on Twitter; @IrwinQWart. You can find him on FaceBook, too!

Irwin Quagmire Wart name and image are copyrighted.

www.ingramcontent.com/pod-product-compliance
Lightning Source LLC
Chambersburg PA
CBHW061054090426
42742CB00002B/34